Cool and Crazy
Engine Aircraft Automobile Machines,

Exploded Diagrams

Cut Away Diagrams

To COLOR

Twenty plus pictures to browse generate
Ideas, projects, education,

Color them to relax,

Some are exploded

Some are cutaways

Some are partially colored to start.
Locomotives, Formula 1 Cars,

Airplanes, Fighter Planes

Helicopter,

Evan a Starship

RELAX, ENJOY, COLOR!!!!!

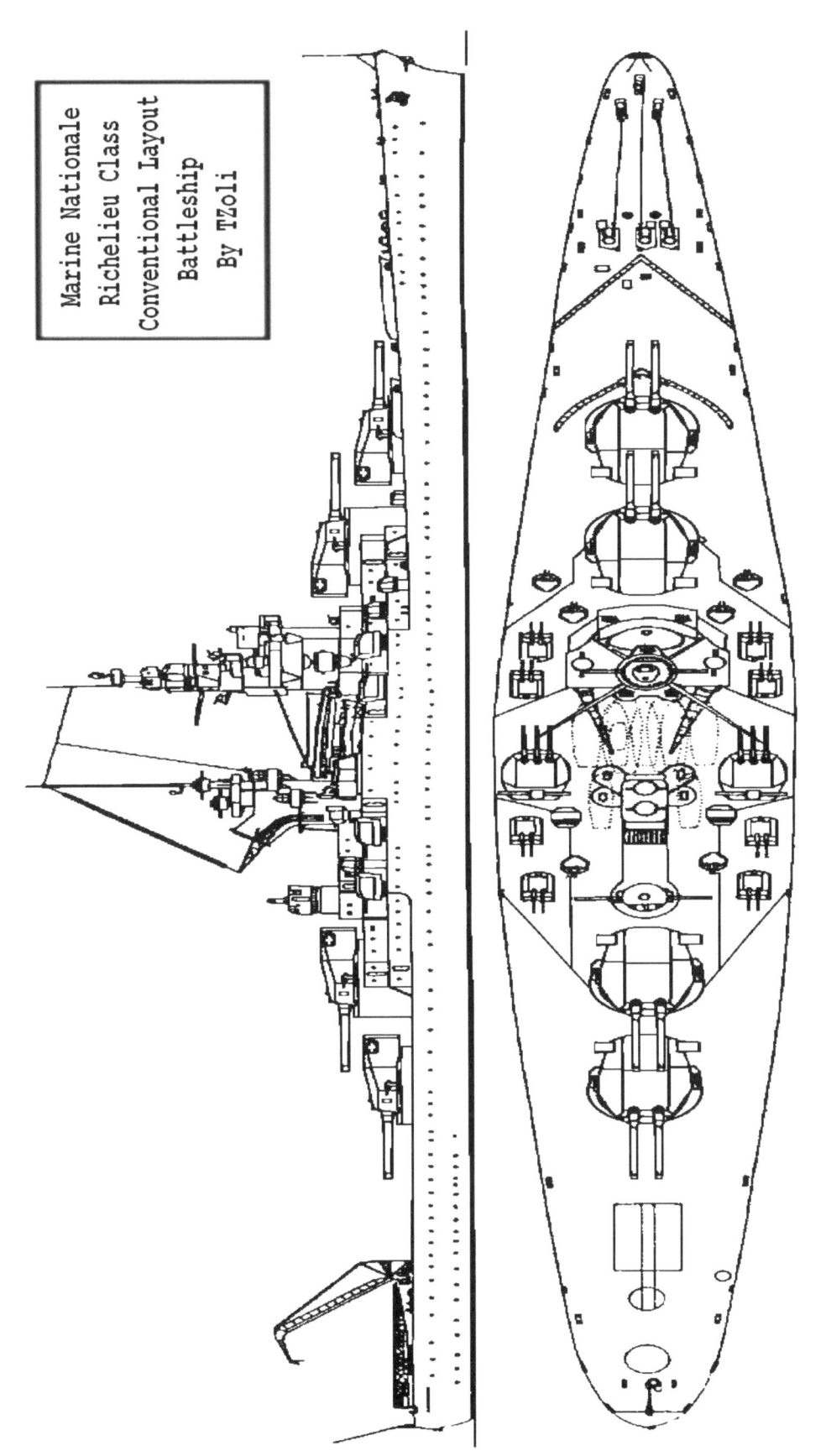

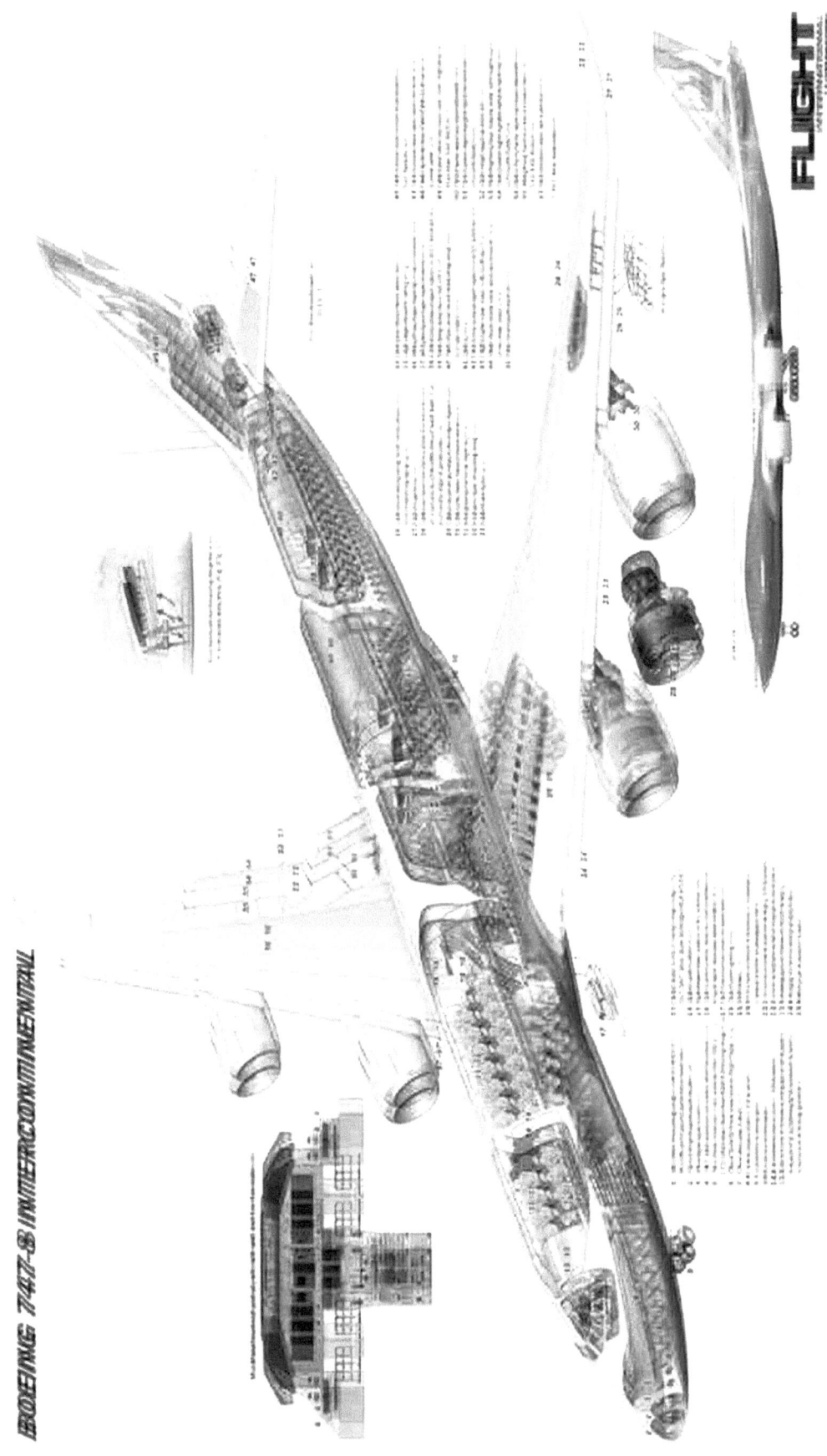

PROTOTYPE
Audi R8 S V8 Coupé
Abmessungen
Dimensions
02/12

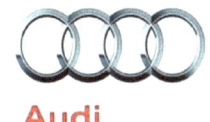

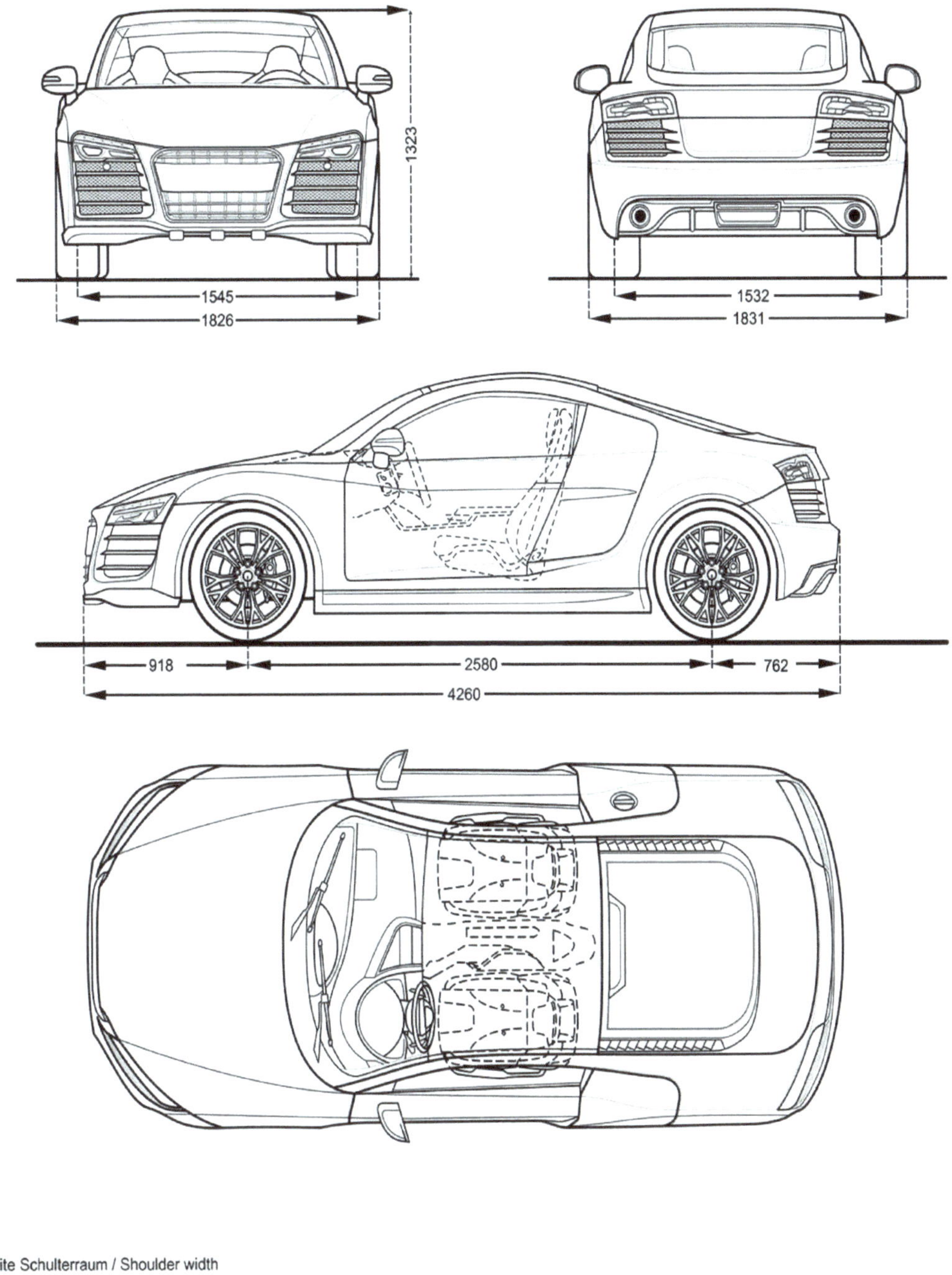

1 Breite Schulterraum / Shoulder width
2 Breite Ellbogenraum / Elbow width
*maximaler Kopfraum / Maximum headroom
Angaben Millimeter / Dimensions in milimeters
Angabe der Abmessungen bei Fahrzeugleergewicht / Dimensions of vehicle unloaded
Details Größe ist ungefähr / detail size is approximate

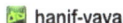 hanif-yayan
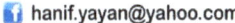 hanif.yayan@yahoo.com

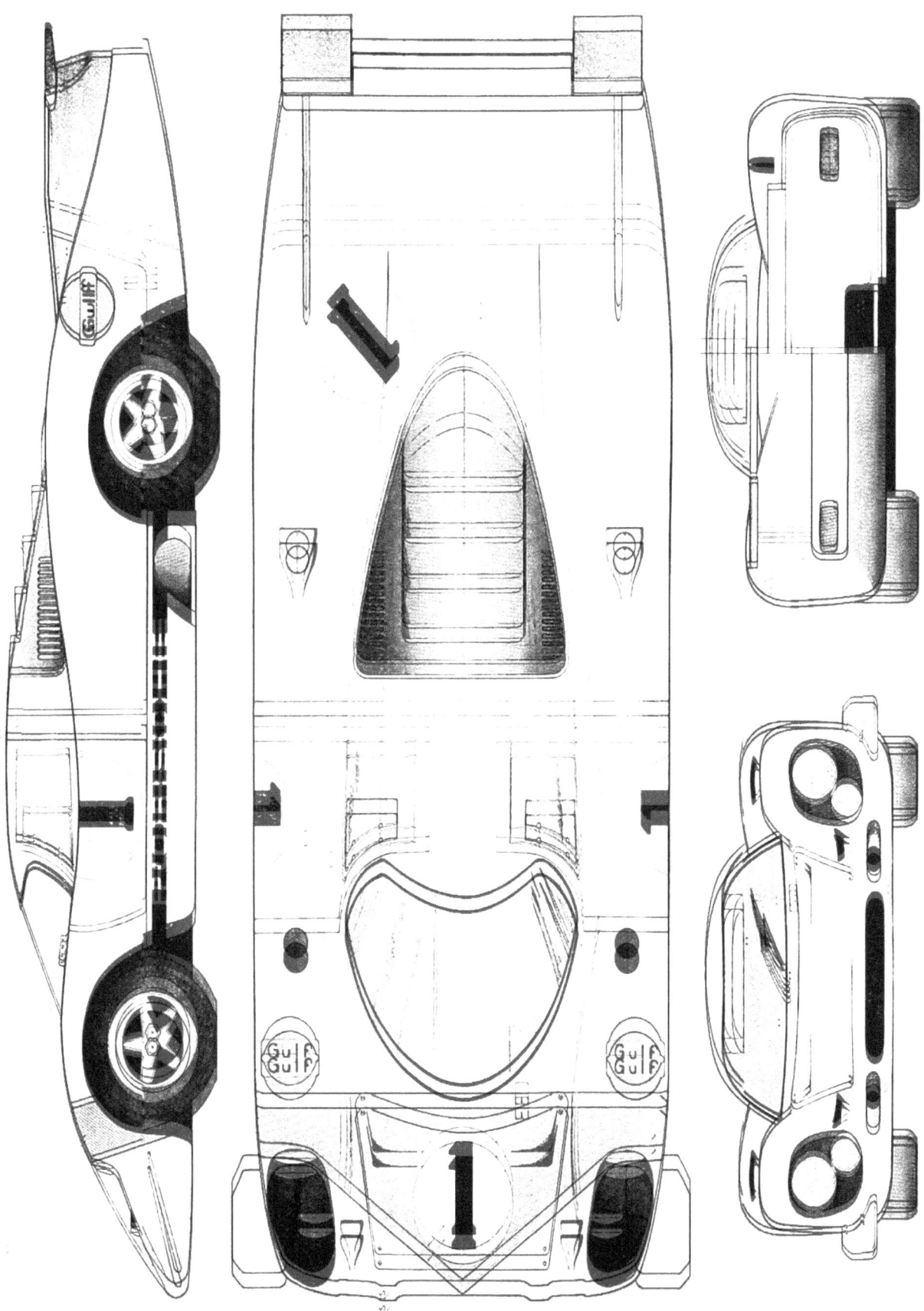

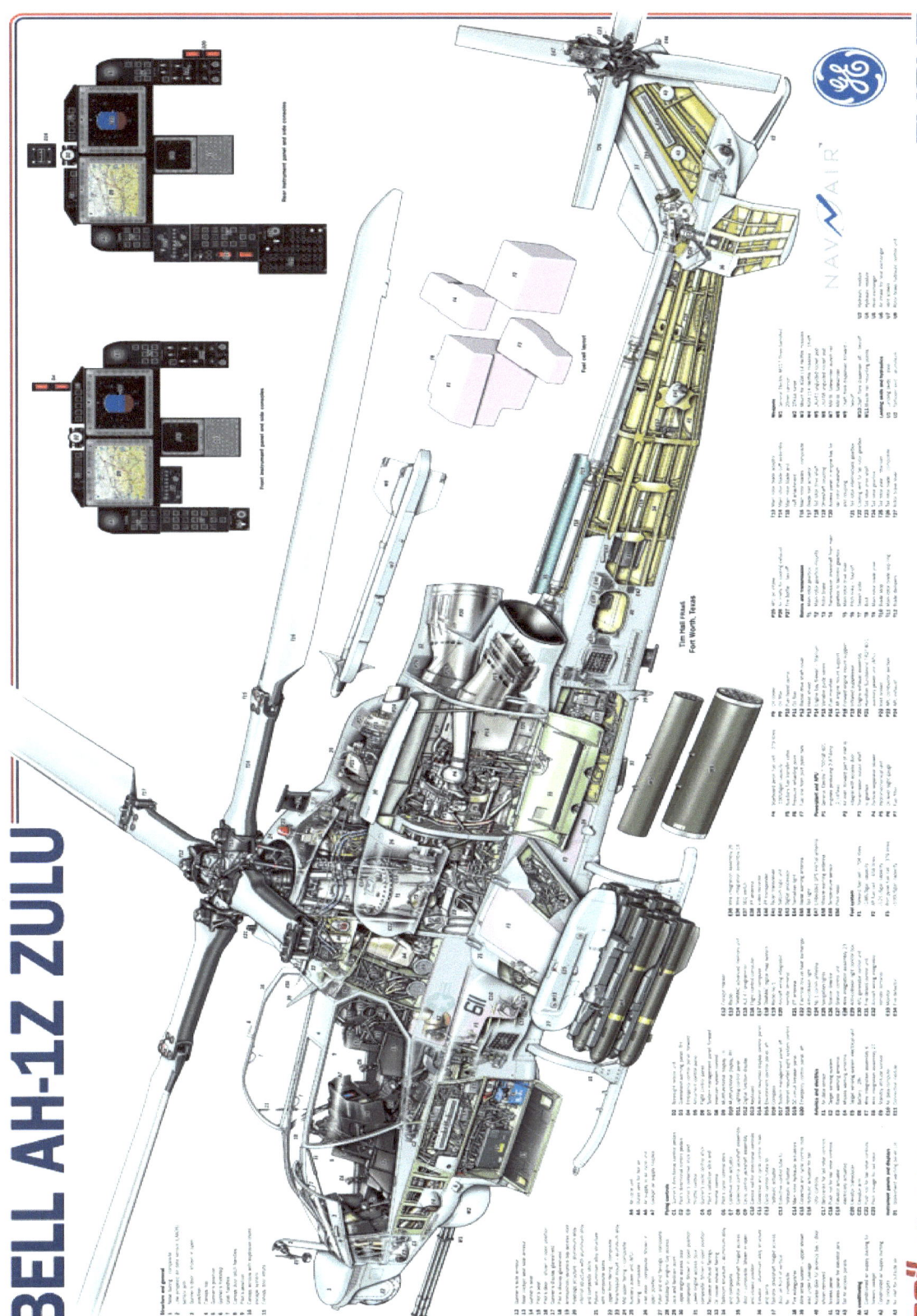

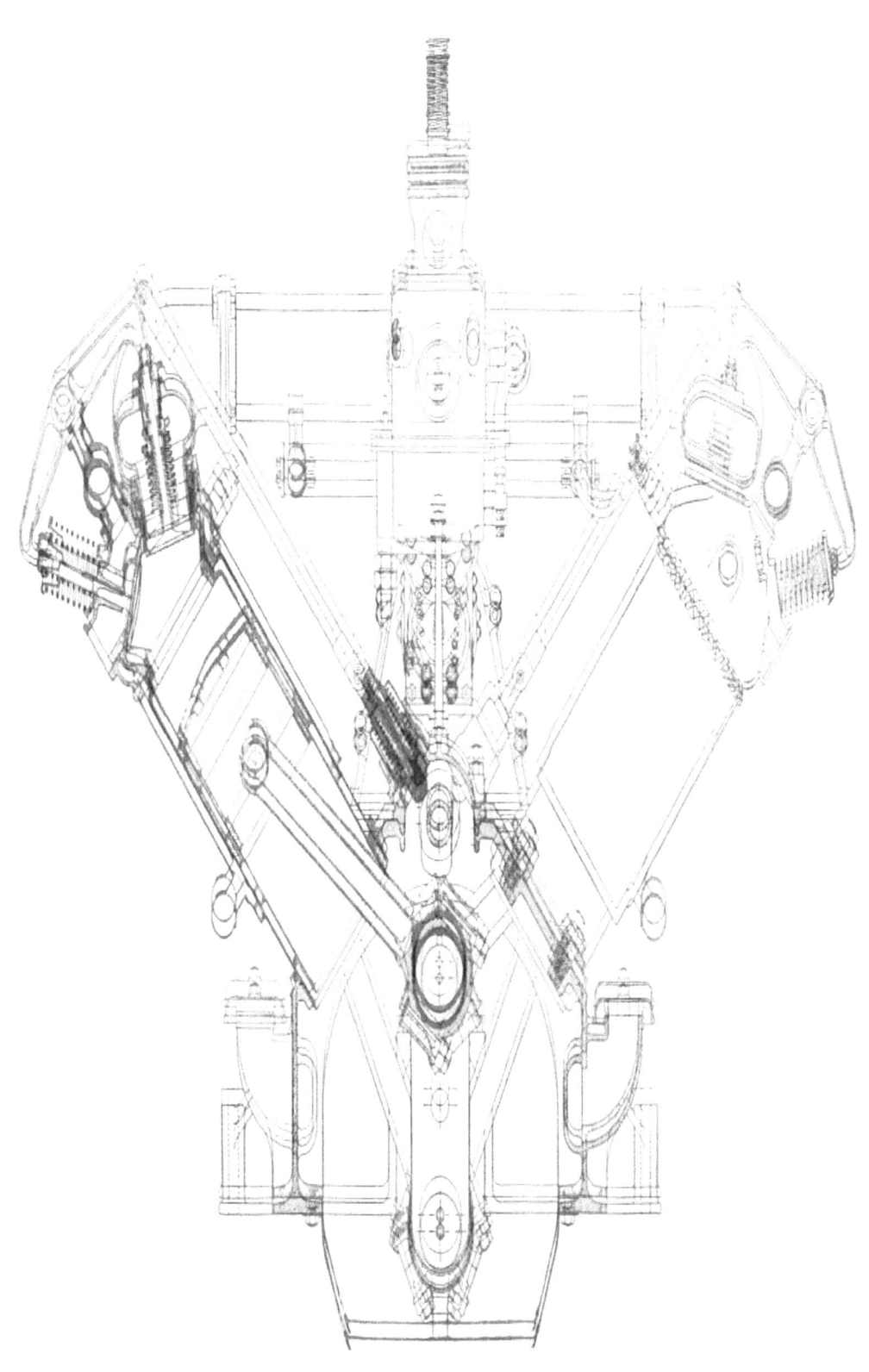

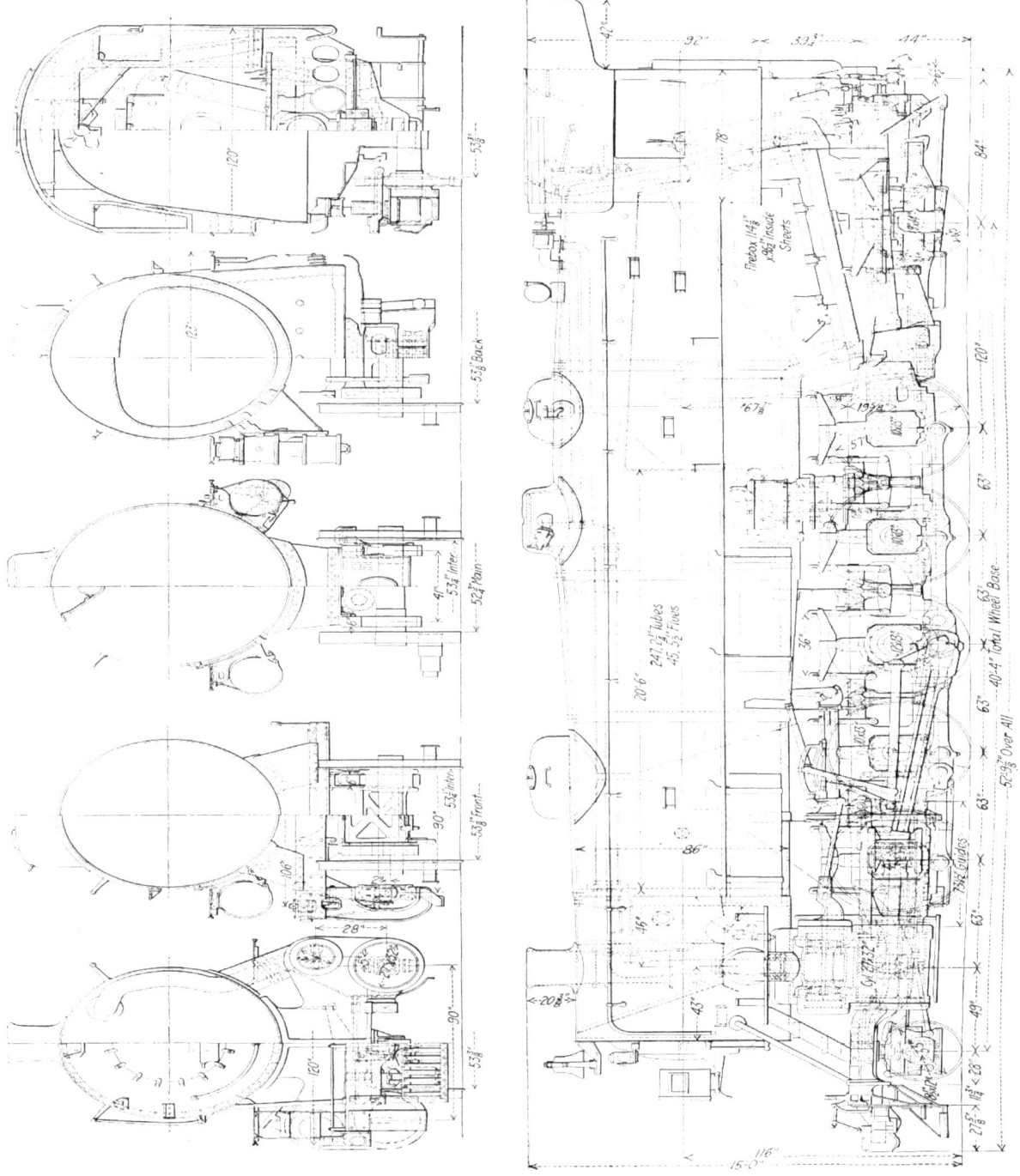

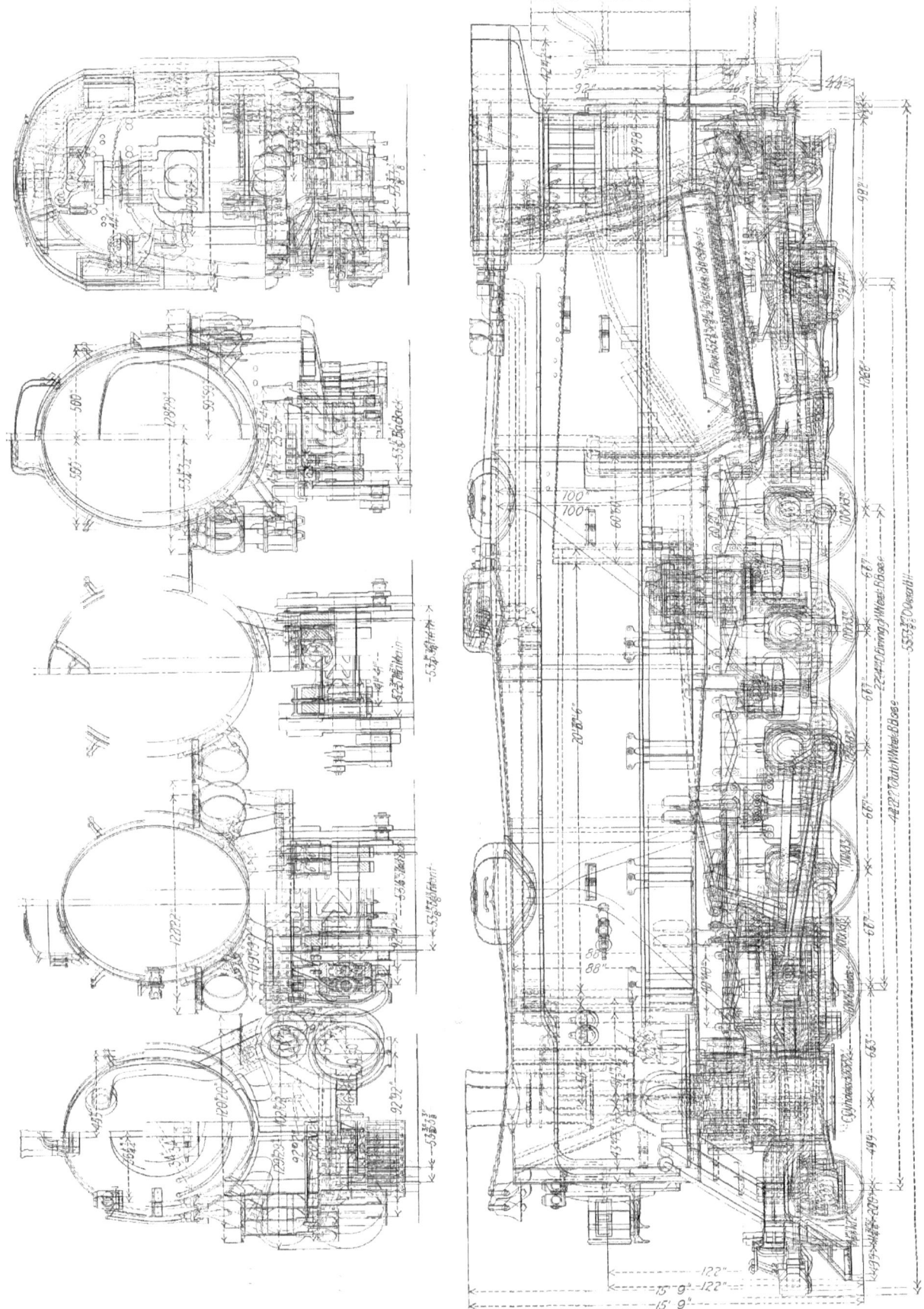

CONSTITUTION CLASS STARSHIP U.S.S. ENTERPRISE NCC-1701
PORT SIDE ELEVATION/PROFILE VIEW MID-LINE INTERNAL ARRANGEMENT

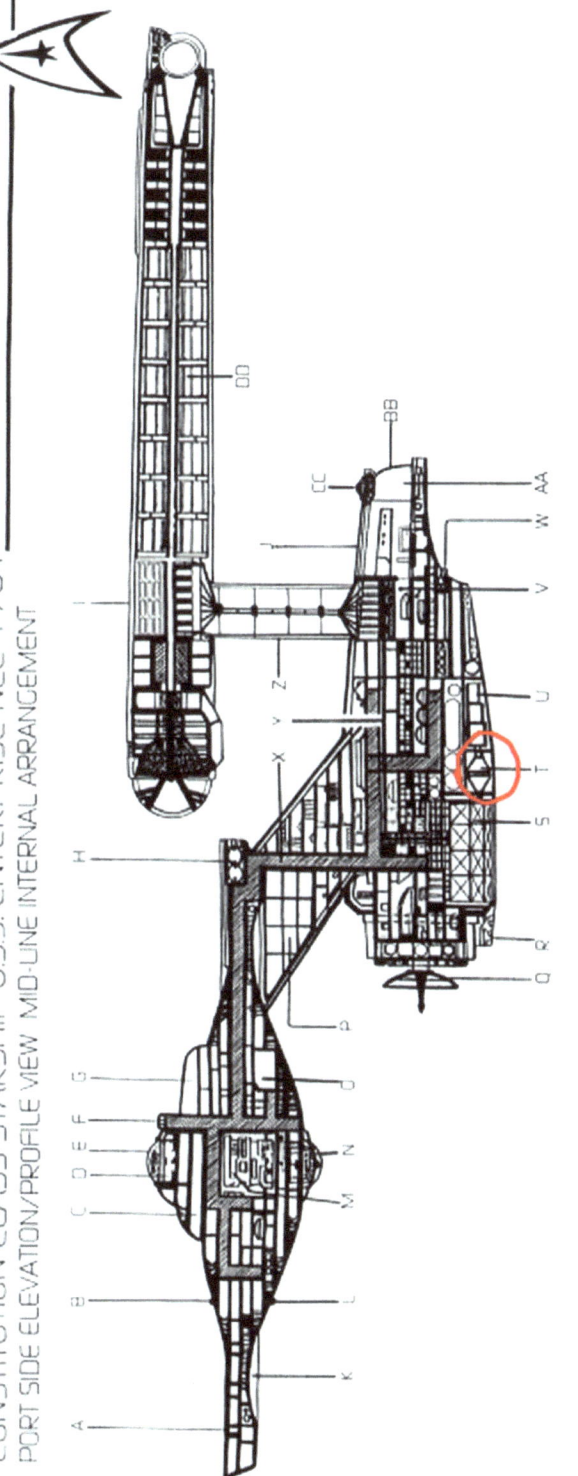

- A   PRIMARY HULL
- B   UPPER PHASER ARRAY (TYP)
- C   FWD TORPEDO BAY
- D   MAIN BRIDGE
- E   UPPER SENSOR ARRAY
- F   TURBO LIFT TUBE DOCKING PASS-THROUGH CONNECTION POINT
- G   AFT TORPEDO BAY
- H   IMPULSE ENGINES
- I   WARP ENGINE NACELLE
- J   SECONDARY/ENGINEERING HULL
- K   PRIMARY HULL UNDERCUT
- L   LOWER PHASER ARRAY (TYP)
- M   MAIN COMPUTER CORE
- N   LOWER SENSOR ARRAY
- O   CARGO HOLD (TYP)
- P   DEUTERIUM TANKAGE
- Q   PRIMARY SCANNER ARRAY
- R   PRIMARY DOCKING HARD POINTS (3)
- S   ANTIMATTER CONTAINMENT VESSELS
- T   MAIN M/AM POWER TAPS
- U   EMERGENCY POWER SYSTEMS
- V   SHUTTLE WORK BAYS
- W   AFT TRACTOR BEAM EMITTER
- X   TURBO LIFT TUBE (TYP)
- Y   MAIN ENGINE FLUX TRANSFER CONDUIT
- Z   WARP ENGINE SUPPORT NACELLE (2)
- AA MAIN SHUTTLE LANDING BAY
- BB SHUTTLE BAY DOORS
- CC AFT SENSOR ARRAY
- DD WARP COILS

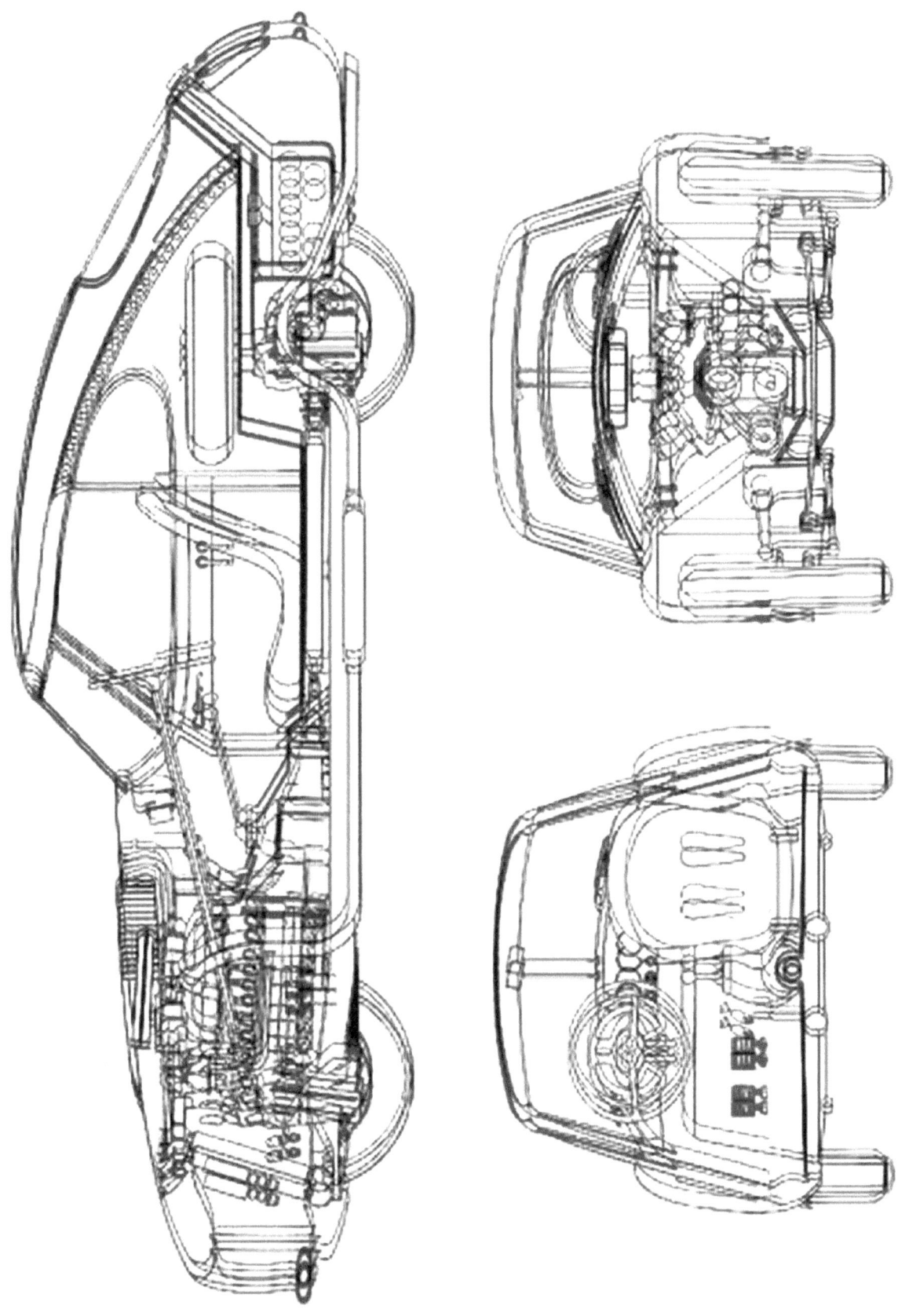

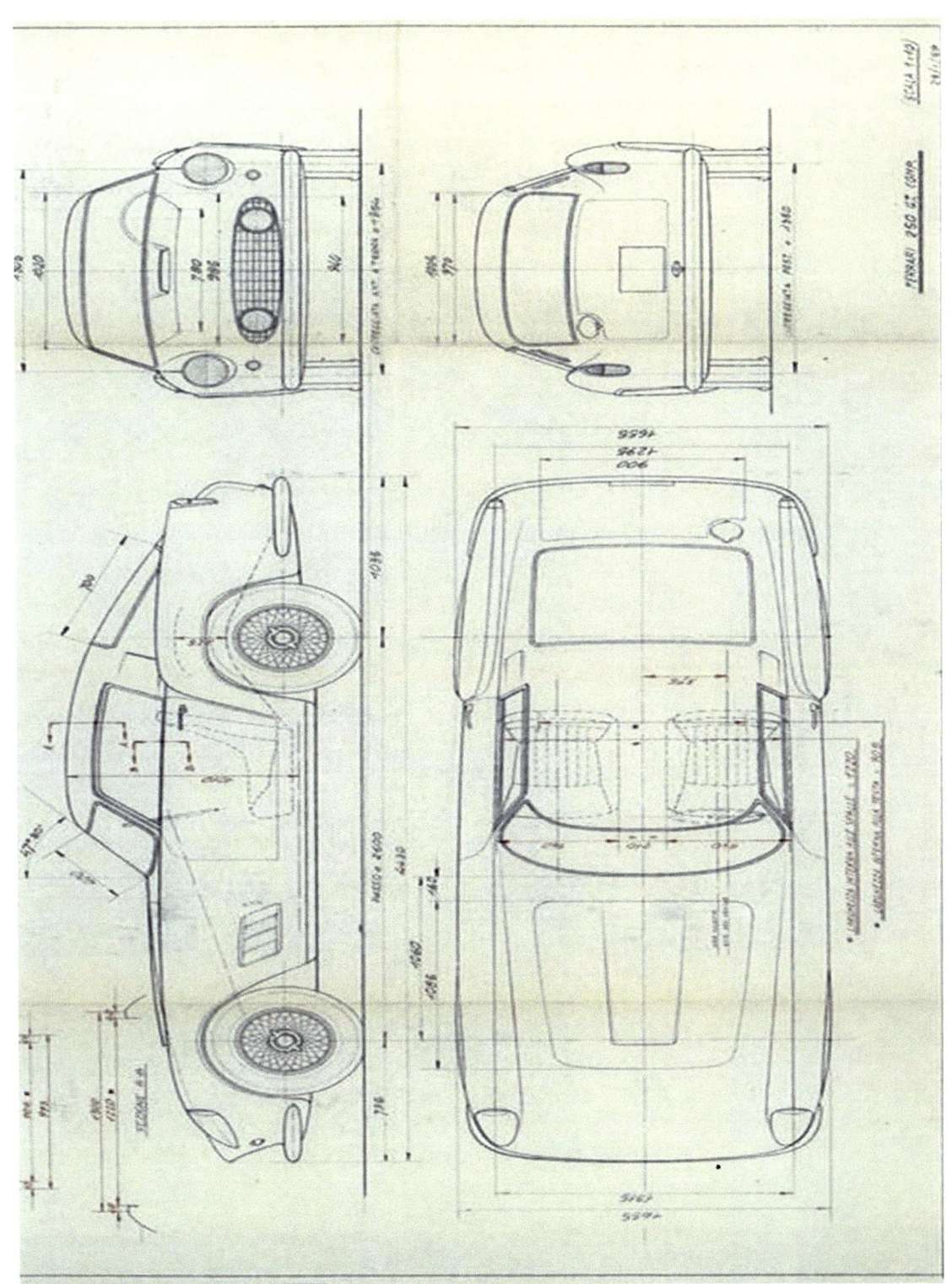

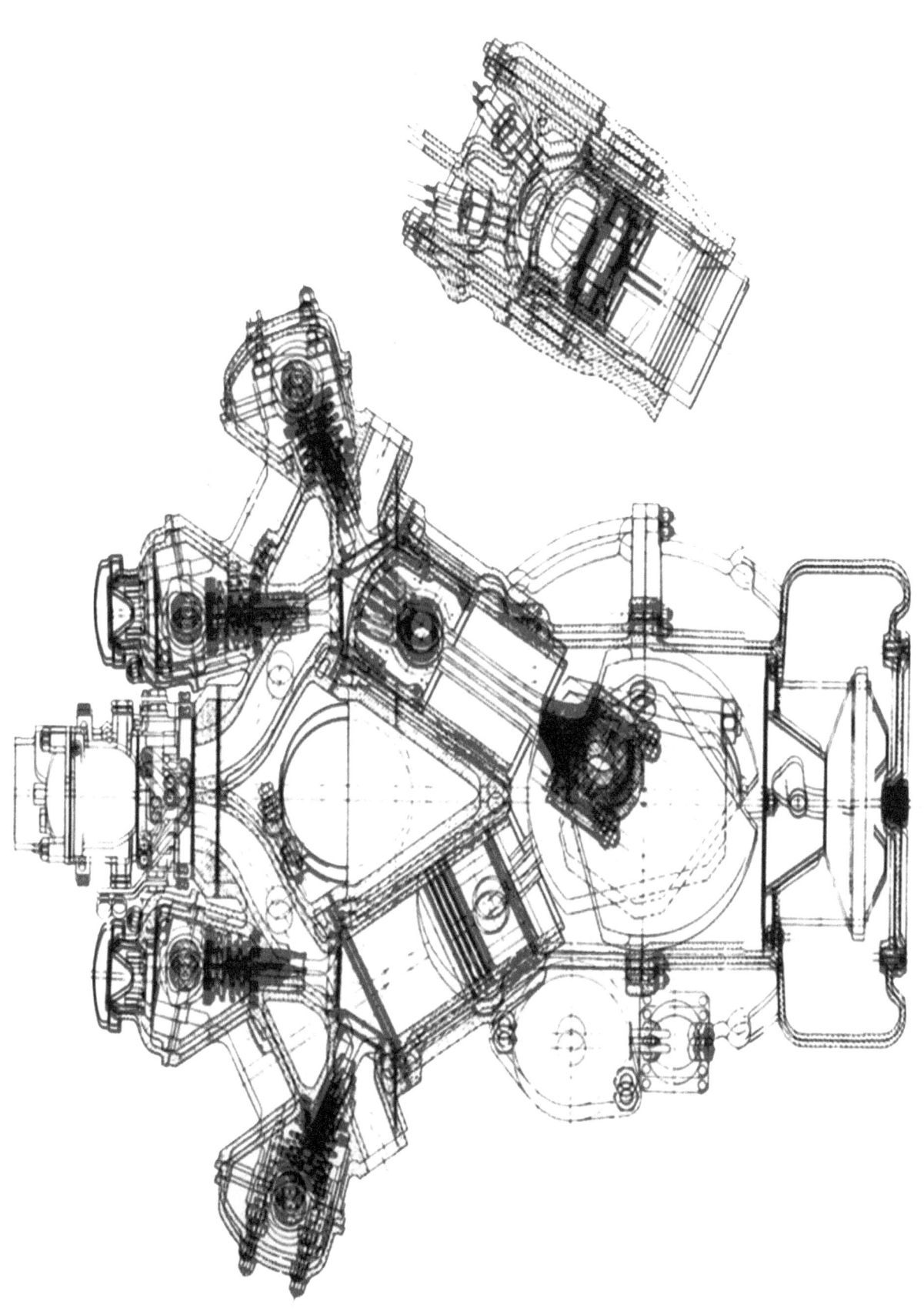

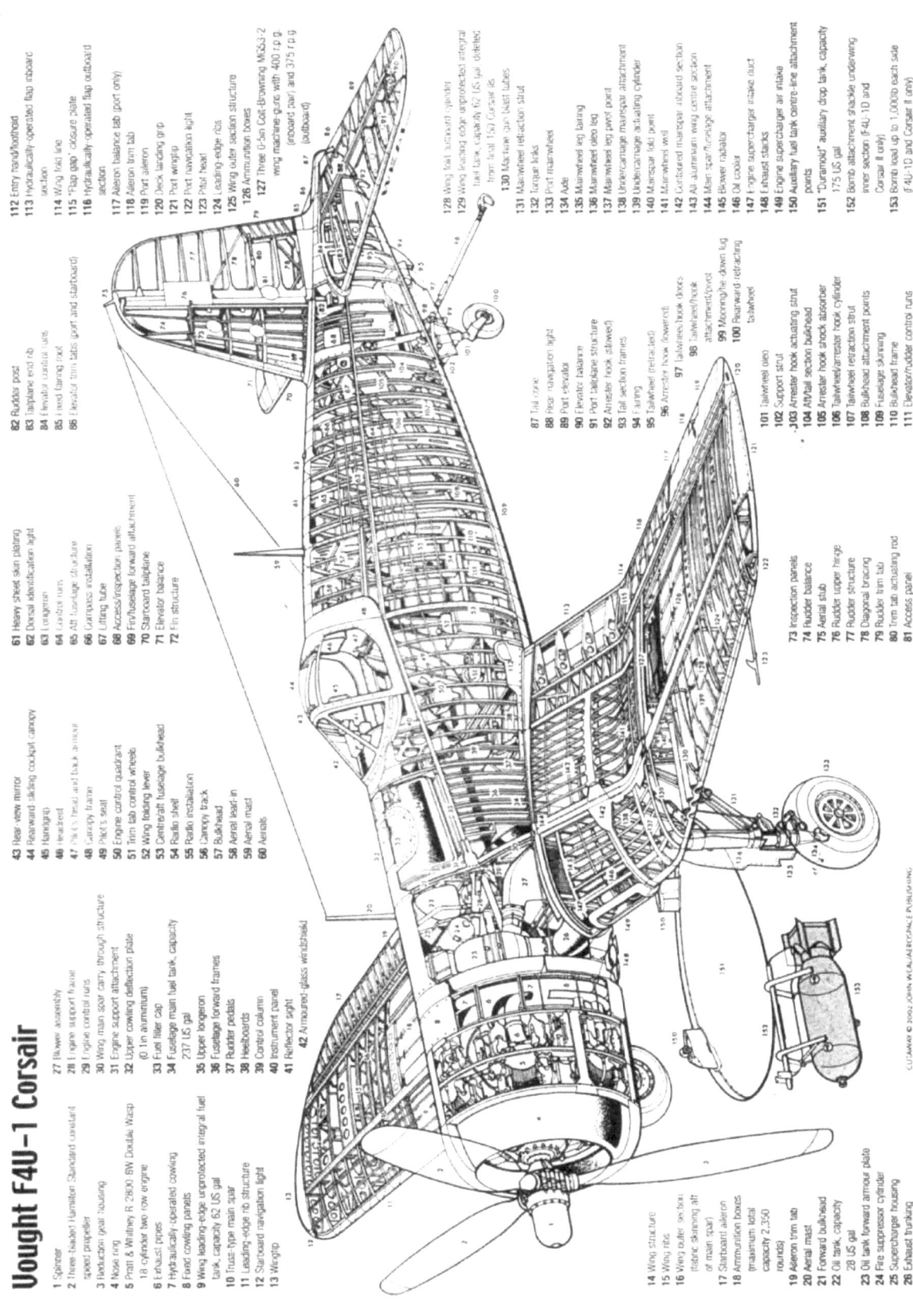

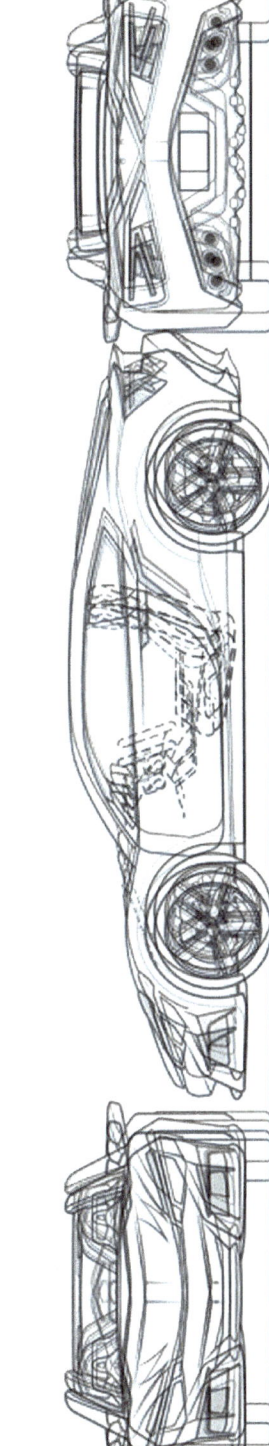
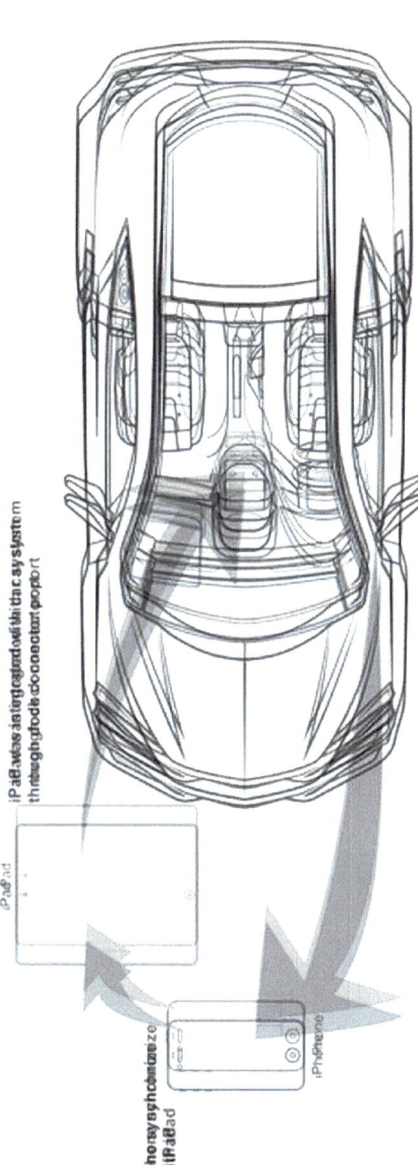

PROTOTYPE
HONDA S2 iDrive design

Dimensions
02/04/12

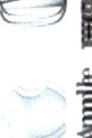

iPad commands dictated out of the car via the connected or in the car system through the dock connector port

iPhone syncs/charges within iPad

All commands dictated out of the car via the connected or in the car system through the dock connector port

iPad
iPhone

1) 肩幅 / Shoulder width
2) 肘幅 / Elbow width
3) 車内ベッド リリース / Maximum hiproom
Dimensions of vehicle should be in millimeters

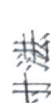
hhanfiypypym
hhanfiypypm@yahoo.com

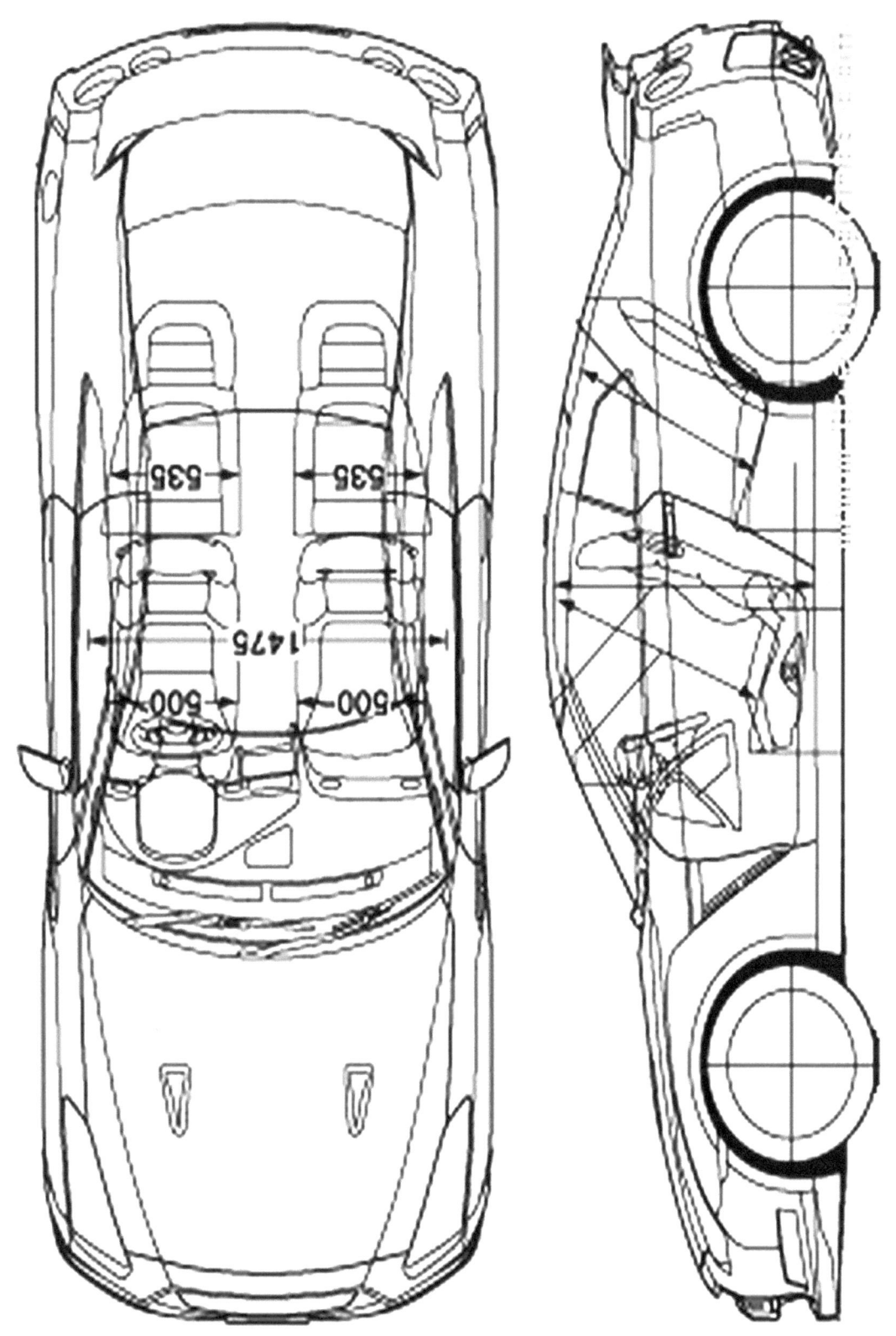

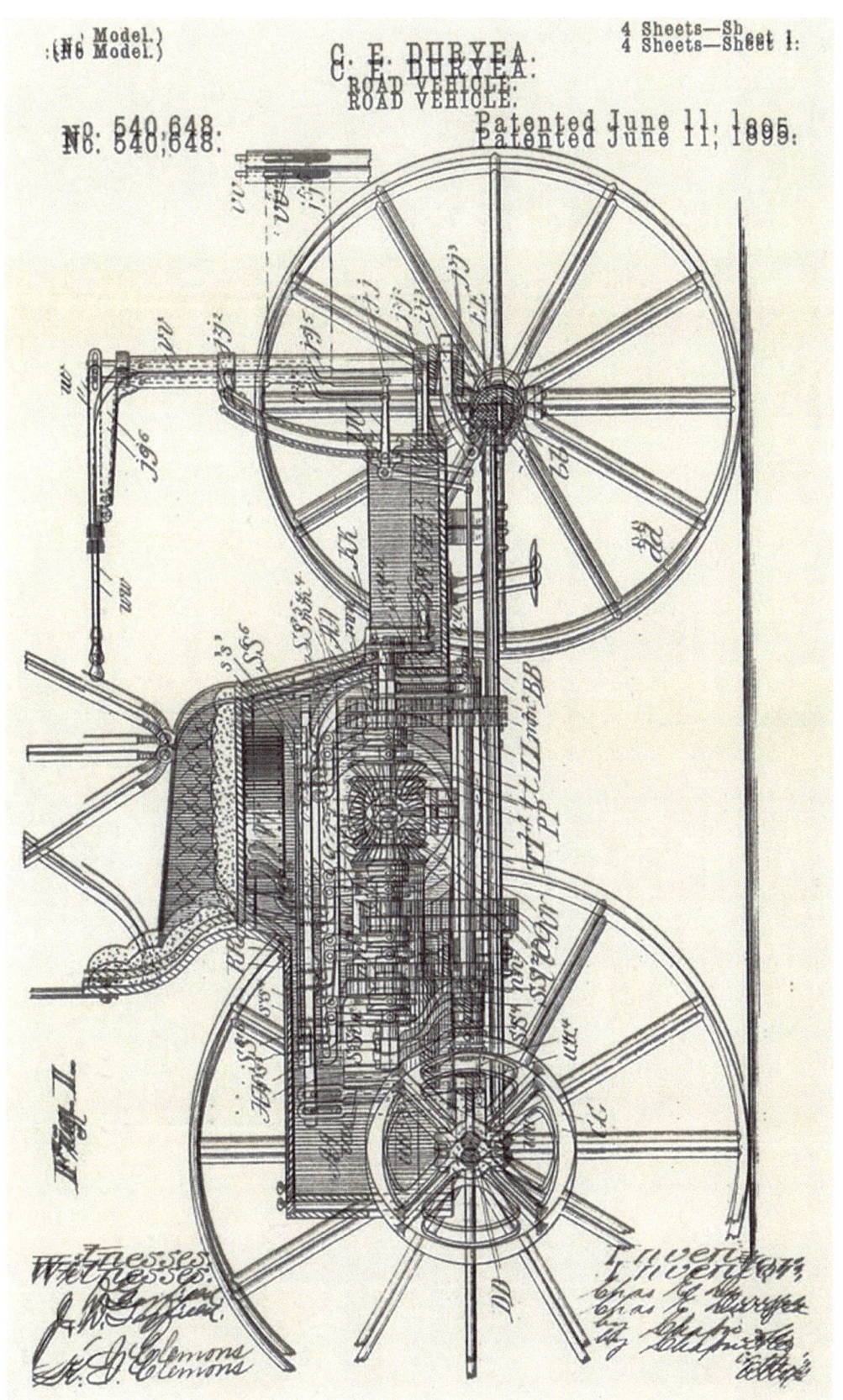

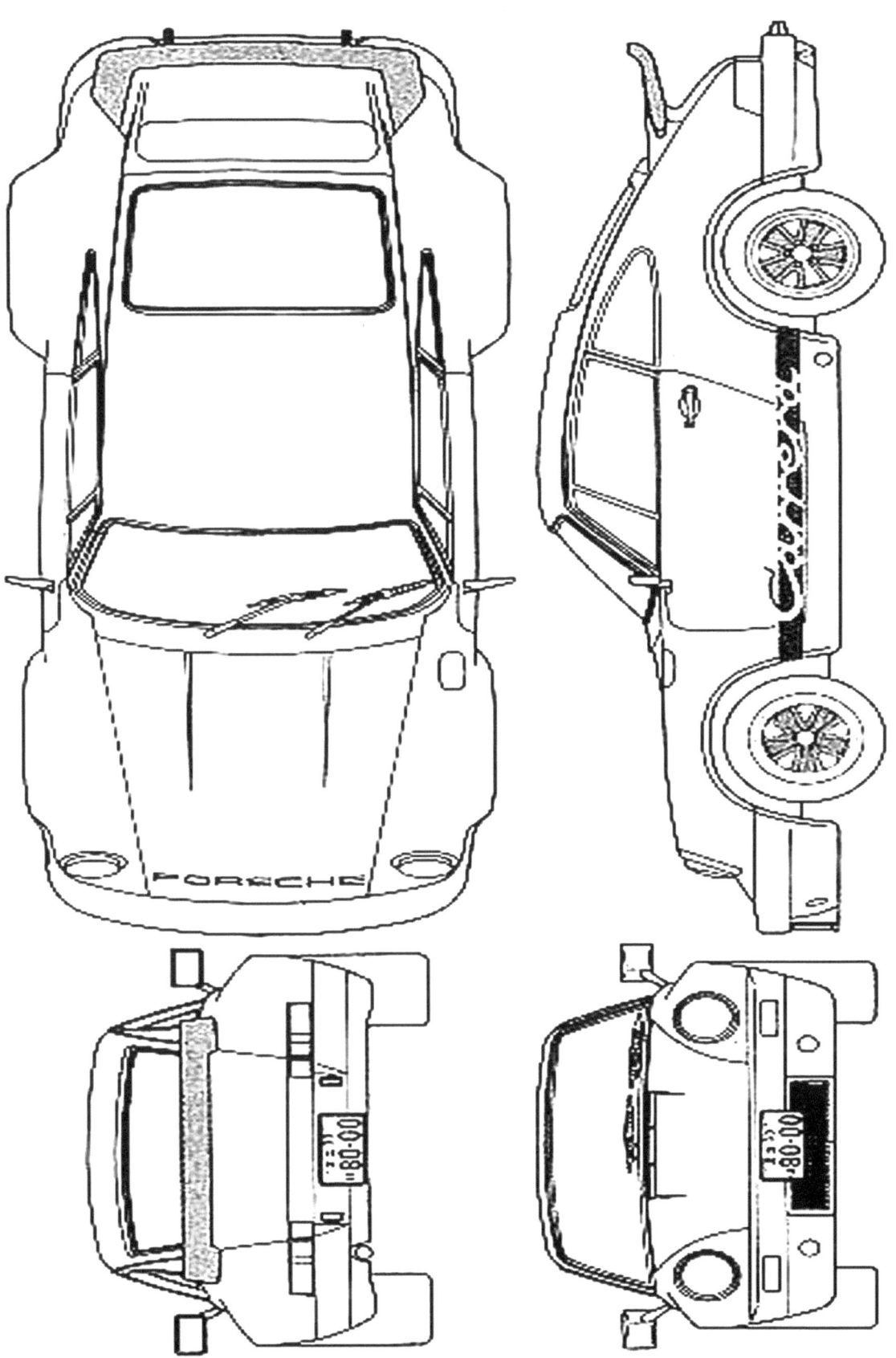

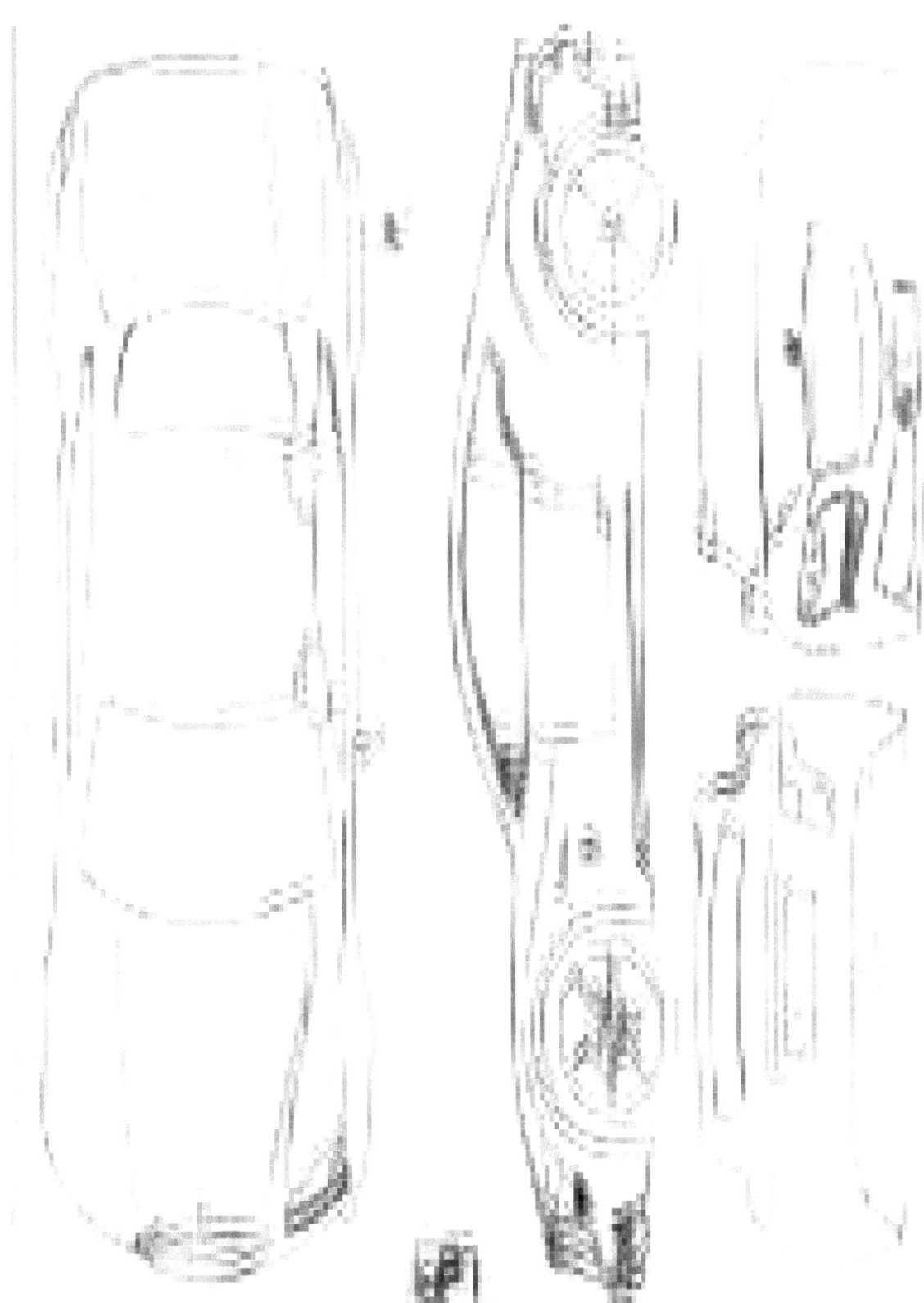

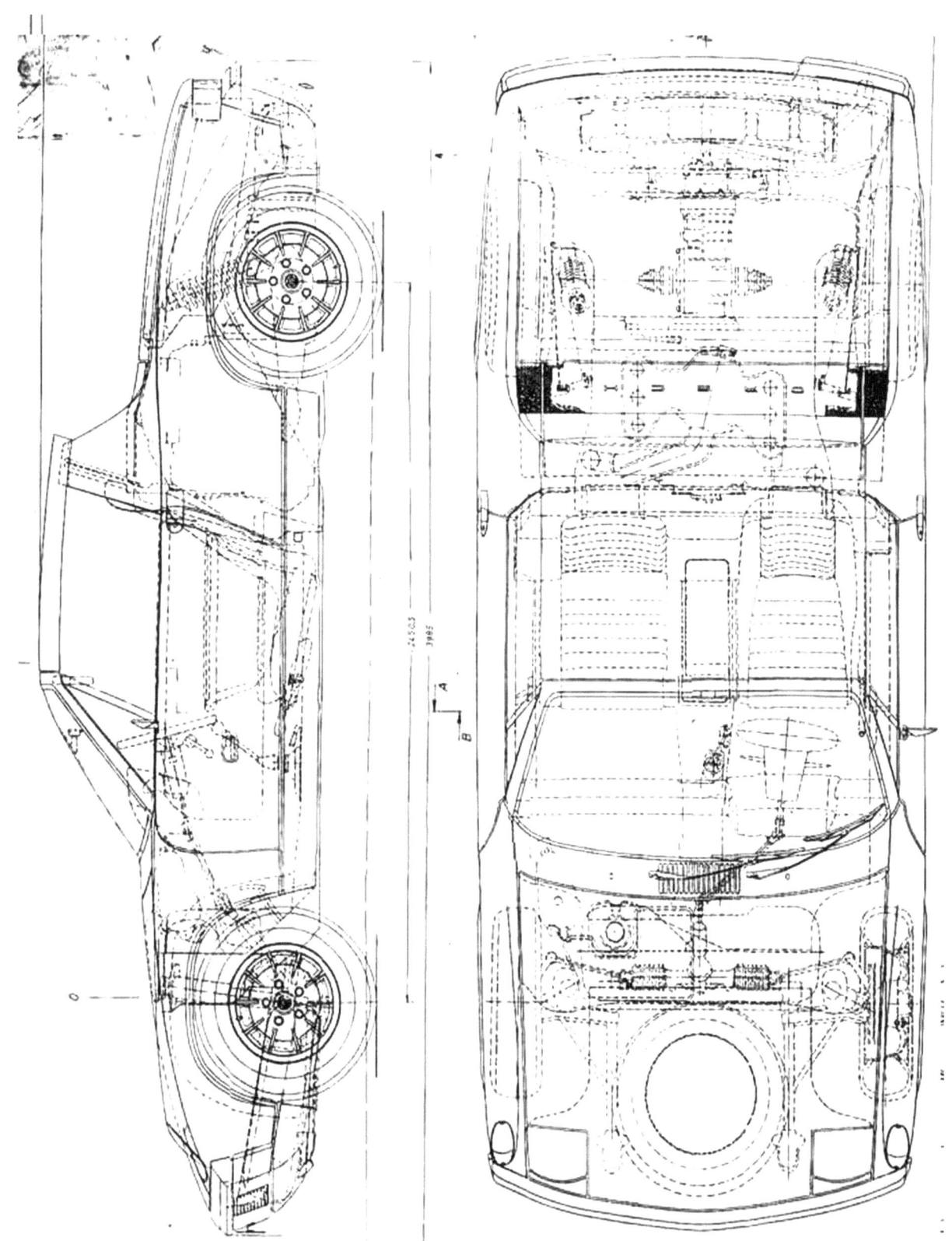

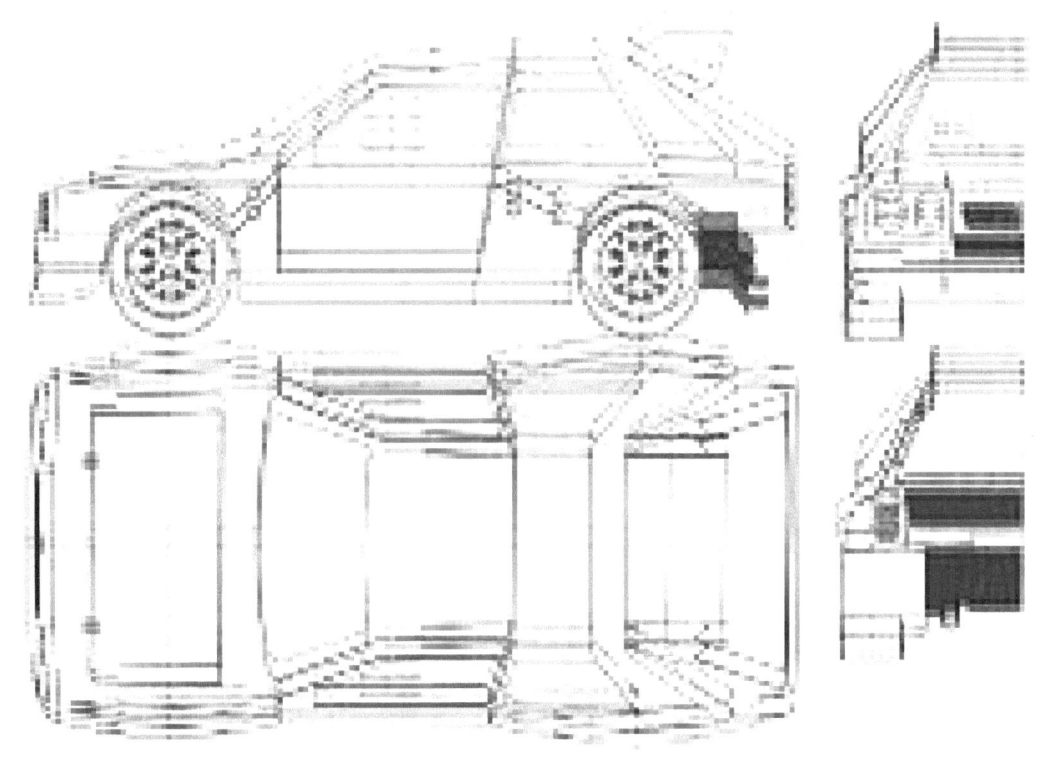
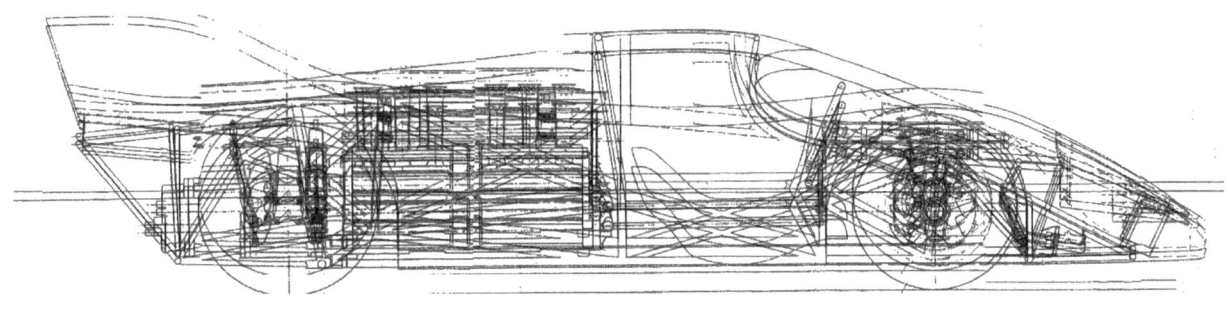

THANK YOU
FOR COLORING
NAILHEADMETALPUNK

www.ingramcontent.com/pod-product-compliance
Lightning Source LLC
Chambersburg PA
CBHW051930210526
45473CB00006B/2202